Connected  Mathematics™

Accentuate the Negative

Integers

Student Edition

Glenda Lappan
James T. Fey
William M. Fitzgerald
Susan N. Friel
Elizabeth Difanis Phillips

D1365120

PEARSON

Prentice
Hall

Needham, Massachusetts
Upper Saddle River, New Jersey

Connected Mathematics™ was developed at Michigan State University with the support of National Science Foundation Grant No. MDR 9150217.

This project was supported, in part,
by the
National Science Foundation
Opinions expressed are those of the authors
and not necessarily those of the Foundation

The Michigan State University authors and administration have agreed that all MSU royalties arising from this publication will be devoted to purposes supported by the Department of Mathematics and the MSU Mathematics Education Enrichment Fund.

Photo Acknowledgements: 14 © Esbin-Anderson/The Image Works; 29 © Mike Douglas/The Image Works; 30 © Michael Dwyer/Stock, Boston; 34 © Peter Menzel/Stock, Boston; 46 © Alan Carey/The Image Works; 50 © Superstock, Inc.; 63 © Superstock, Inc.; 65 © Barbara Van Cleve/Tony Stone Images

ISBN 0-13-180818-4
3 4 5 6 7 8 9 10   07 06 05 04

The Connected Mathematics Project Staff

Project Directors

James T. Fey
University of Maryland

William M. Fitzgerald
Michigan State University

Susan N. Friel
University of North Carolina at Chapel Hill

Glenda Lappan
Michigan State University

Elizabeth Difanis Phillips
Michigan State University

Project Manager

Kathy Burgis
Michigan State University

Technical Coordinator

Judith Martus Miller
Michigan State University

Curriculum Development Consultants

David Ben-Chaim
Weizmann Institute

Alex Friedlander
Weizmann Institute

Eleanor Geiger
University of Maryland

Jane Mitchell
University of North Carolina at Chapel Hill

Anthony D. Rickard
Alma College

Collaborating Teachers/Writers

Mary K. Bouck
Portland, Michigan

Jacqueline Stewart
Okemos, Michigan

Graduate Assistants

Scott J. Baldridge
Michigan State University

Angie S. Eshelman
Michigan State University

M. Faaiz Gierdien
Michigan State University

Jane M. Keiser
Indiana University

Angela S. Krebs
Michigan State University

James M. Larson
Michigan State University

Ronald Preston
Indiana University

Tat Ming Sze
Michigan State University

Sarah Theule-Lubienski
Michigan State University

Jeffrey J. Wanko
Michigan State University

Evaluation Team

Mark Hoover
Michigan State University

Diane V. Lambdin
Indiana University

Sandra K. Wilcox
Michigan State University

Judith S. Zawojewski
National-Louis University

Teacher/Assessment Team

Kathy Booth
Waverly, Michigan

Anita Clark
Marshall, Michigan

Julie Faulkner
Traverse City, Michigan

Theodore Gardella
Bloomfield Hills, Michigan

Yvonne Grant
Portland, Michigan

Linda R. Lobue
Vista, California

Suzanne McGrath
Chula Vista, California

Nancy McIntyre
Troy, Michigan

Mary Beth Schmitt
Traverse City, Michigan

Linda Walker
Tallahassee, Florida

Software Developer

Richard Burgis
East Lansing, Michigan

Development Center Directors

Nicholas Branca
San Diego State University

Dianne Briars
Pittsburgh Public Schools

Frances R. Curcio
New York University

Perry Lanier
Michigan State University

J. Michael Shaughnessy
Portland State University

Charles Vonder Embse
Central Michigan University

Special thanks to the students and teachers at these pilot schools!

Baker Demonstration School
Evanston, Illinois

Bertha Vos Elementary School
Traverse City, Michigan

Blair Elementary School
Traverse City, Michigan

Bloomfield Hills Middle School
Bloomfield Hills, Michigan

Brownell Elementary School
Flint, Michigan

Catlin Gabel School
Portland, Oregon

Cherry Knoll Elementary School
Traverse City, Michigan

Cobb Middle School
Tallahassee, Florida

Courtade Elementary School
Traverse City, Michigan

Duke School for Children
Durham, North Carolina

DeVeaux Junior High School
Toledo, Ohio

East Junior High School
Traverse City, Michigan

Eastern Elementary School
Traverse City, Michigan

Eastlake Elementary School
Chula Vista, California

Eastwood Elementary School
Sturgis, Michigan

Elizabeth City Middle School
Elizabeth City, North Carolina

Franklinton Elementary School
Franklinton, North Carolina

Frick International Studies Academy
Pittsburgh, Pennsylvania

Gundry Elementary School
Flint, Michigan

Hawkins Elementary School
Toledo, Ohio

Hilltop Middle School
Chula Vista, California

Holmes Middle School
Flint, Michigan

Interlochen Elementary School
Traverse City, Michigan

Los Altos Elementary School
San Diego, California

Louis Armstrong Middle School
East Elmhurst, New York

McTigue Junior High School
Toledo, Ohio

National City Middle School
National City, California

Norris Elementary School
Traverse City, Michigan

Northeast Middle School
Minneapolis, Minnesota

Oak Park Elementary School
Traverse City, Michigan

Old Mission Elementary School
Traverse City, Michigan

Old Orchard Elementary School
Toledo, Ohio

Portland Middle School
Portland, Michigan

Reizenstein Middle School
Pittsburgh, Pennsylvania

Sabin Elementary School
Traverse City, Michigan

Shepherd Middle School
Shepherd, Michigan

Sturgis Middle School
Sturgis, Michigan

Terrell Lane Middle School
Louisburg, North Carolina

Tierra del Sol Middle School
Lakeside, California

Traverse Heights Elementary School
Traverse City, Michigan

University Preparatory Academy
Seattle, Washington

Washington Middle School
Vista, California

Waverly East Intermediate School
Lansing, Michigan

Waverly Middle School
Lansing, Michigan

West Junior High School
Traverse City, Michigan

Willow Hill Elementary School
Traverse City, Michigan

Contents

Accentuate the Negative

On Tuesday, a cold front passed through, causing the temperature to change ⁻2°F per hour from noon until 10:00 A.M. the next morning. The temperature at noon on Tuesday was 75°F. What was the temperature at 4:00 P.M. Tuesday?

If a negative number is subtracted from a negative number, then the difference is a negative number. *Decide whether this statement is always true, sometimes true, or always false. Give examples to illustrate your thinking.*

In the first quarter of the big game, the Littleton Lions gain 5 yards on every play. They are now on their own 25-yard line. On what yard line were the Lions three plays ago?

Most of the numbers you have worked with in math class this year have been greater than or equal to 0. However, many times numbers less than 0 can provide important information. Winter temperatures in many places fall below 0°. Businesses that lose money report profits less than $0. Scores for professional golfers are often reported as numbers less than 0, indicating the number of strokes under par.

Numbers greater than 0 are called **positive numbers**, and numbers less than 0 are called **negative numbers**. In *Accentuate the Negative*, you will work with both positive and negative numbers. In particular, you will study a set of numbers called the integers, and you will explore models that help you think about adding, subtracting, multiplying, and dividing positive and negative integers.

As you work through the investigations in this unit, you will solve problems like those on the opposite page.

Mathematical Highlights

In *Accentuate the Negative* you will develop understanding of and algorithms for operations with integers. The unit should help you to:

- Compare and order integers;

- Represent integers on a number line;

- Understand the relationship between an integer and its inverse and the absolute value of numbers;

- Develop ways to model sums, differences, and products of integers, including number line models and chip models;

- Develop strategies and algorithms for adding, subtracting, multiplying, and dividing integers;

- Model situations and solve problems using integers;

- Graph in four quadrants; and

- Graph linear equations using a graphing calculator to observe the effects of changing a coefficient to its inverse or adding a constant to $y = ax$.

As you work the problems in this unit, make it a habit to ask yourself questions about situations that involve integers: *What quantities in the problem can be represented with positive and negative numbers? How can you tell which of two integers is the greater? What models or diagrams might help decide which operation is useful in solving a problem? What is the approximate answer to the computation?*

Extending the Number Line

In math class this year, you have worked with numbers greater than or equal to 0. Numbers greater than 0 are called *positive numbers*. You can write a positive number with a plus sign, as in +150, with a raised plus sign, as in $^+150$, or without a plus sign, as in 150. For example, a temperature of 10 degrees above zero can be written +10°, $^+10°$, or 10°.

Often we need to talk about numbers less than 0. For example, on a very cold day, the temperature might drop below 0°. A company may spend more money than it earns and report a profit less than $0. Numbers less than 0 are called **negative numbers**. You can write a negative number with a minus sign, as in −150, or with a raised minus sign, as in $^-150$. For example, a temperature of 10 degrees below zero can be written −10° or $^-10°$.

Did you know?

You have probably seen golf scores reported with negative numbers. A golf hole is assigned a value called par. *Par* is the number of strokes a skilled golfer might take to reach the hole. For example, a skilled golfer should be able to complete a par-4 hole in four strokes. If a golfer completes a par-4 hole in six strokes, then her score for the hole could be reported as $^+2$, or "two over par." If a golfer completes a par-4 hole in two strokes, her score for the hole could be reported as $^-2$, or "two under par." Some scores for a hole are given special names. A score of $^+1$ is a *bogey*, a score of $^-1$ is a *birdie*, and a score of $^-2$ is an *eagle*. A player's score for a round of golf can be reported as the total number of strokes she is above or below par for the entire course.

1.1 Playing MathMania

Ms. Bernoski's third-period class is playing MathMania, a game similar to the *Jeopardy!*® game show. The game board is shown below. The top row gives six math categories. Below each category name are five cards. The front of each card shows a point value, and the back of each card has a question related to the category. Cards with higher point values have more difficult questions.

Operations with fractions	Similarity	Probability	Area and perimeter	Tiling the plane	Factors and multiples
50	50	50	50	50	50
100	100	100	100	100	100
150	150	150	150	150	150
200	200	200	200	200	200
250	250	250	250	250	250

The game is played by teams. One team starts the game by choosing a category and a point value. The teacher asks the question on the back of the corresponding card. The first team to answer the question correctly gets the point value on the card, and the card is removed from the board. If a team misses the question, the point value is subtracted from their score. The team that answers correctly gets to choose the next category and point value.

At one point in the game, the scores for Ms. Bernoski's class are as follows:

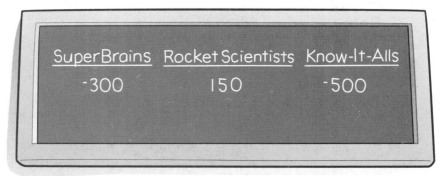

SuperBrains	RocketScientists	Know-It-Alls
⁻300	150	⁻500

There are several ways each team could have reached their score. For example, to earn their 150 points, the Rocket Scientists may have answered a 100-point question and a 50-point question correctly, or they may have answered a 200-point question correctly and then missed a 50-point question.

Problem 1.1

A. Which team has the highest score? Which team has the lowest score? Explain how you know your answers are correct.

B. How many points separate the highest score and the lowest score?

C. The discussion above describes two possible ways the Rocket Scientists may have reached their score. Describe another possible way. For each of the other two teams, give one possible way the team could have reached their score.

After achieving the scores shown above, the teams continue to play the game. Here is what happens:

- The SuperBrains answer a 200-point question correctly, a 150-point question incorrectly, a 50-point question correctly, and another 50-point question correctly.

- The Rocket Scientists answer a 50-point question incorrectly, a 200-point question incorrectly, a 100-point question correctly, and a 150-point question incorrectly.

- The Know-It-Alls answer a 100-point question incorrectly, a 200-point question correctly, a 150-point question correctly, and a 50-point question incorrectly.

D. What is each team's score now?

E. Which team is in last place? How far behind each of the other two teams is this team?

■ Problem 1.1 Follow-Up

In Ms. Bernoski's fifth-period class, the Smarties have $^-300$ points, and the Brain Surgeons have $^-150$ points. After answering the next four questions, the Smarties are tied with the Brain Surgeons. Give two possible ways the Smarties could have done this.

1.2 **Winning the Game**

At the end of the MathMania game, the scoreboard looks like this:

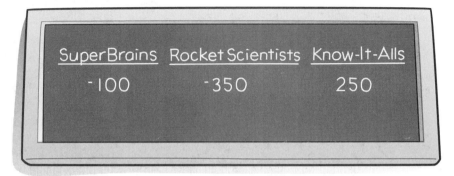

The Know-It-Alls are the winners because they have the highest score. The Rocket Scientists are in last place because they have the lowest score. The SuperBrains are in second place because they have a lower score than the Know-It-Alls but did not lose as many points as the Rocket Scientists. You can write this as

-350 is less than -100, which is less than 250.

Or, you can use symbols to write

$$^-350 < {}^-100 < 250$$

Problem 1.2

Mr. Hazan plays MathMania with his class. He divides the class into five teams. At the end of the game, the scores are as follows:

Team A: 200   Team B: -250   Team C: -400   Team D: 350   Team E: -100

A. Order the teams by score, from first place through fifth place.

B. By how many points is the first-place team ahead of the second-place team?

C. By how many points is the first-place team ahead of the third-place team?

D. By how many points is the second-place team ahead of the fourth-place team?

E. By how many points is the third-place team ahead of the fifth-place team?

1. Copy each pair of numbers below, inserting > or < to make a true statement.

   a. 53   35   **b.** ⁻50   0   **c.** ⁻30   15   **d.** ⁻70   ⁻90

2. Order the numbers below from least to greatest.

   25, 2, 5, ⁻3, 15, ⁻7, ⁻25, 12, 1, ⁻4, 0

1.3 Measuring Temperature

You have used the number line to help you think about whole numbers and fractions and decimals greater than 0. These are all examples of positive numbers. The number line can be extended to the left of 0 to include negative numbers.

A thermometer can be thought of as a vertical number line with the positive numbers above 0 and the negative numbers below 0. The temperature in many places falls below 0° during the winter months. The thermometer below shows a temperature reading of ⁻4°F:

Problem 1.3

A. Arrange the following temperatures in order from lowest to highest:

⁻8°, 4°, 12°, ⁻2°, 0°, ⁻15°

B. The temperature reading on a thermometer is 5°F. Tell what the new reading will be if the temperature

   1. rises 10°   **2.** falls 2°   **3.** falls 10°   **4.** rises 7°

C. The temperature reading on a thermometer is ⁻5°F. Tell what the new reading will be if the temperature

   1. falls 3°   **2.** rises 3°   **3.** falls 10°   **4.** rises 10°

D. In 1–6, give the temperature halfway between the two given temperatures.

   1. 0° and 10°   **2.** ⁻5° and 15°   **3.** 5° and ⁻15°
   4. 0° and ⁻20°   **5.** ⁻8° and 8°   **6.** ⁻6° and ⁻16°

E. In 1–4, tell which temperature reading is farther from ⁻2°.

   1. ⁻6° or 6°   **2.** ⁻7° or 3°   **3.** 2° or ⁻5°   **4.** ⁻10° or 5°

F. Explain how you determined your answer for part 4 of question E.

■ Problem 1.3 Follow-Up

The numbers ⁻3 and 3 are represented on the number line below.

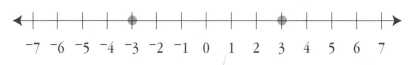

Notice that both numbers are 3 units from 0, but 3 is to the right of 0, and ⁻3 is to the left of 0.

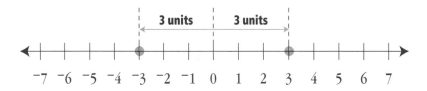

The numbers ⁻3 and 3 are called opposites. **Opposites** are numbers that are the same distance from 0 but on different sides of 0. If you folded the number line at 0, each number would match up with its opposite.

If a team playing the MathMania game starts with 0 points and then answers a 50-point question correctly, they will have ⁺50 points. If they miss the question, they will have ⁻50 points. The numbers ⁺50 and ⁻50 are opposites: they are the same distance from 0 on the number line, but in different directions. The sign of a number tells its direction from 0.

1. Give the opposite of each number.
   a. ⁻7   **b.** 18   **c.** ⁻42   **d.** 0

2. Name two numbers on the number line that are the same distance from ⁻2. Are these numbers opposites?

At the end of Mr. Hazan's MathMania game, the scores of the five teams are as follows:
Team A: ⁻50   Team B: 150   Team C: ⁻300   Team D: 0   Team E: 100

3. Order the teams from first place through fifth place.

4. Draw a number line. Mark and label each team's score. Label the point for each team with both the team letter and the score.

5. On the number line, what is the distance between the scores of Team A and Team B?

6. On the number line, what is the distance between the scores of Team C and Team A?

7. On the number line, what is the distance between the scores of Team D and Team E?

8. Tell how each team, by answering one question, could change their score to 0. Give the point value of the question, and tell whether the team must answer the question correctly or incorrectly. If this is not possible for a particular team, explain why.

As you work on these ACE questions, use your calculator whenever you need it.

Applications

In 1–3, tell what the MathMania team's score would be after the events described. Assume the team starts with 0 points.

1. The Protons answer a 250-point question correctly, a 100-point question correctly, a 200-point question correctly, a 150-point question incorrectly, and a 200-point question incorrectly.

2. The Neutrons answer a 200-point question incorrectly, a 50-point question correctly, a 250-point question correctly, a 150-point question incorrectly, and a 50-point question incorrectly.

3. The Electrons answer a 50-point question incorrectly, a 200-point question incorrectly, a 100-point question correctly, a 200-point question correctly, and a 150-point question incorrectly.

In 4–7, a MathMania score is given. Describe a sequence of five events that would produce the score.

4. 300 **5.** ⁻200 **6.** ⁻250 **7.** 0

8. a. Draw a number line, and mark and label points for the following numbers:

⁻10, ⁻15, 18, ⁻5, 8, 0, 15, ⁻1

Use your number line to help you with parts b–f.

b. What is the opposite of 18?

c. What is the opposite of ⁻10?

d. Find a number greater than ⁻5.

e. Find a number less than ⁻15.

f. Which numbers are 6 units from ⁻2?

In 9–14, copy the pair of numbers, inserting > or < to make a true statement.

9. 3   0

10. ⁻23   25

11. 46   ⁻79

12. ⁻75   ⁻90

13. ⁻300   100

14. ⁻1000   ⁻999

In 15–17, give the distance between the two numbers on the number line.

15. 53 and 35

16. ⁻50 and ⁻90

17. ⁻30 and 15

In 18–20, use the thermometer shown to help you answer the questions. The thermometer shows temperatures on the Celsius temperature scale. On this scale, 0°C is the freezing point of water.

18. What is the temperature change from ⁻12°C to ⁺13°C?

19. What is the temperature change from ⁺32°C to ⁺12°C?

20. What is the temperature change from ⁺8°C to ⁻7°C?

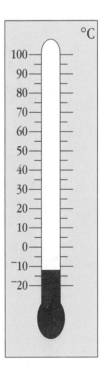

21. Copy the table below. Study the first two rows, and then complete the table.

Temperature at 9:00 A.M.	Temperature at 9:00 P.M.	Change in temperature from 9:00 A.M. to 9:00 P.M.
−3°	5°	8°
5°	−3°	−8°
−10°	3°	
−2°	−10°	
−13°	−5°	
2°	−12°	
−10°		−7°
	6°	15°
−2°		−10°

22. The highest temperature ever recorded in the United States was 56.7°C (about 134°F) in Death Valley, California, on July 10, 1913. The lowest recorded U.S. temperature was −62.2°C (about −80°F) in Prospect Creek, Alaska, on January 23, 1971.

a. In Celsius degrees, what is the difference between the record high and record low temperatures?

b. In Fahrenheit degrees, what is the difference between the record high and record low temperatures?

Connections

23. In MathMania, winning 100 points and then losing 100 points have the effect of "undoing" each other. In other words, since they are opposites, 100 and −100 combine to give 0. Describe three real-life situations in which two events undo each other.

In 24 and 25, copy the number line below. Mark and label the number line to show the approximate locations of the numbers given.

24. $-\frac{2}{3}, {}^+\frac{2}{5}, -1.5, {}^+1\frac{3}{4}$ **25.** $-1.25, -\frac{1}{3}, {}^+1.5, -\frac{1}{6}$

26. The list below gives average temperatures (in °C) for Fairbanks, Alaska, for each month of the year from January through December.

$-25, -20, -13, -2, {}^+9, {}^+15, {}^+17, {}^+14, {}^+7, -4, -16, -23$

  a. What is the median of these monthly temperatures?

  b. What is the range of these monthly temperatures (lowest to highest)?

Extensions

27. At the start of December, Shareef has a balance of $595.50 in his checking account. The following is a list of transactions he makes during the month.

Date	Transaction	Balance
December 1		$595.50
December 5	Writes a check for $19.95	
December 12	Writes a check for $280.88	
December 15	Deposits $257.00	
December 17	Writes a check for $58.12	
December 21	Withdraws $50	
December 24	Writes checks for $17.50, $41.37, and $65.15	
December 26	Deposits $100	
December 31	Withdraws $50	

  a. What is Shareef's balance at the end of December?

  b. On what day is his balance greatest? On what day is his balance least?

28. In the first quarter of the big game, the Littleton Lions gain 5 yards on every play. They are now on their own 25-yard line.

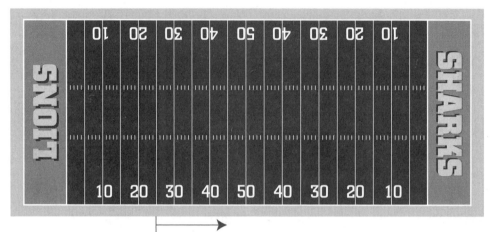

The Lions are here now and are moving from left to right—
that is, they move right when they gain yards.

a. On what yard line were the Lions three plays ago?

b. On what yard line will they be after the next two plays?

29. In the last quarter of the big game, the Littleton Lions (see question 28) lose 5 yards on every play. They are now on their own 25-yard line. They move left when they lose yards.

a. On what yard line were the Lions two plays ago?

b. On what yard line will they be after the next two plays?

Mathematical Reflections

In this investigation, you worked with positive and negative numbers. You analyzed sequences of events in the MathMania game, looked at temperature, and extended the number line to represent numbers less than 0. You also learned how to decide whether one number is less than or greater than another number. These questions will help you summarize what you have learned:

1 Describe what positive numbers, negative numbers, and 0 mean in terms of

   a. keeping score in MathMania.

   b. temperature readings.

2 Describe how you can compare the following types of numbers to decide which is greater. Use examples to illustrate your thinking.

   a. two positive numbers

   b. two negative numbers

   c. a positive number and a negative number

3 Describe how to locate numbers on a number line. Use examples to illustrate your thinking. Be sure to include positive and negative numbers as well as fractions and decimals in your examples.

Think about your answers to these questions, discuss your ideas with other students and your teacher, and then write a summary of your findings in your journal.

Adding Integers

The numbers 0, 1, 2, 3, 4, . . . are *whole numbers*. These numbers are labeled on the number line below.

If we extend this pattern to the left of 0, we get . . . , ⁻4, ⁻3, ⁻2, ⁻1, 0, 1, 2, 3, 4, ...

This larger set of numbers is called the **integers**. The numbers 1, 2, 3, 4, . . . are *positive integers,* and the numbers . . . , ⁻4, ⁻3, ⁻2, ⁻1 are *negative integers.* The number 0 is neither positive nor negative.

In many situations, you need to combine integers to find a sum. In this investigation, you will use two models that will help you think about how to add positive and negative integers.

Did you know?

The Hindus were the first to use negative numbers. The Hindu mathematician Brahmagupta used negative numbers as early as A.D. 628, and even stated the rules for adding, subtracting, multiplying, and dividing with negative numbers. Many European mathematicians of the sixteenth and seventeenth centuries did not accept the idea of negative numbers, referring to them as "absurd" and "fictitious." Mathematicians of that time who did accept negative numbers often had strange beliefs about them. For example, John Wallis believed that negative numbers were greater than infinity!

2.1 Adding on a Number Line

Monique and Ethan were thinking about how to show addition of integers on a number line. They decided to start by working with whole numbers. Monique came up with the following method for representing the **number sentence** 3 + 2 = 5:

Start at 0, and move 3 units to the right. To show the addition of 2, move 2 more units to the right. You end up at 5, so 3 + 2 = 5.

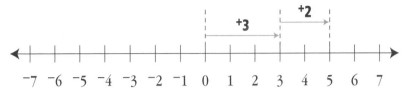

Ethan thought a similar method would work for adding negative integers. He came up with the following plan for finding ⁻3 + ⁻2:

Start at 0, and move 3 units to the left (the negative direction) to represent the ⁻3. To show the addition of ⁻2, move 2 more units to the left. You end up at ⁻5, so ⁻3 + ⁻2 = ⁻5.

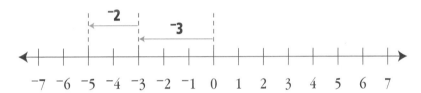

When Ethan wrote ⁻3 + ⁻2 = ⁻5, he used raised negative symbols to help him separate the sign of the integer from the operation sign for addition.

Then, Ethan wanted to try adding a negative integer and a positive integer on a number line. He followed these steps to find ⁻3 + ⁺2:

Start at 0, and move 3 units to the left (the negative direction) to represent ⁻3. To show the addition of ⁺2, move two units to the right (the positive direction). You end up at ⁻1, so ⁻3 + ⁺2 = ⁻1.

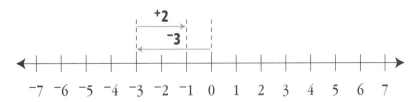

Monique asked Ethan what he thought they would get if they used a number line to find $^+2 + ^-3$. What do you think?

Problem 2.1

A. Write the addition sentence illustrated by each figure.

1.

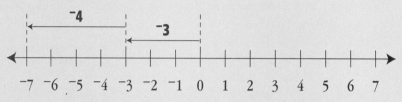

2.

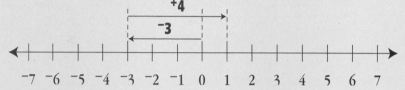

3.

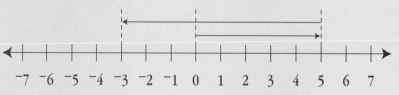

4.

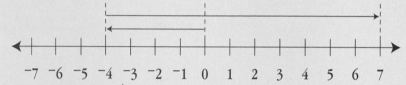

B. Illustrate each addition problem on a number line, and give the answer.

    1. $^-5 + ^+8$ **2.** $^-4 + ^-3$ **3.** $^-2 + ^-3 + ^+10$

C. When you add two integers, does the order of the numbers make a difference? Illustrate your answer by showing each of these pairs of sums on a number line.

    1. $^-5 + ^+10$ and $^+10 + ^-5$ **2.** $^-4 + ^-6$ and $^-6 + ^-4$

    3. $^+8 + ^-8$ and $^-8 + ^+8$ **4.** $^+6 + ^-7$ and $^-7 + ^+6$

Problem 2.1 Follow-Up

1. You can think of the scoring in MathMania as follows: When a team answers a question correctly, a positive integer is added to their score. When a team answers a question incorrectly, a negative integer is added to their score. For each of the following situations, write an addition sentence that will give the team's score. Assume each team starts with 0 points.

   a. The Brainiacs answer a 200-point question correctly and a 150-point question incorrectly.

   b. The Aliens answer a 100-point question correctly and a 100-point question incorrectly.

   c. The Prodigies answer a 50-point question incorrectly, a 100-point question incorrectly, and a 250-point question correctly.

2. Illustrate each addition problem on a number line and give the answer.

   a. $^-2 + {}^+2$ **b.** $^+8 + {}^-8$ **c.** $^-1 + {}^+1$

3. What happens when you add opposites? Explain how you know your answer is correct.

2.2 Inventing a New Model

In the last problem, you used the number line to help you think about adding integers. In this problem, you will explore another way to model the addition of integers.

Amber's mother is an accountant. One day, Amber heard her mother talking to a client on the phone. During the conversation, her mother used the phrases "in the red" and "in the black."

That evening at dinner, Amber asked her mother what these terms meant. Her mother said:

"When people in business talk about income and expenses, they often use colors to describe the numbers they are dealing with. Black refers to profits (or income); red refers to losses (or expenses). A company that is making money, or has money, is 'in the black'; a company that is losing money, or owes money, is 'in the red.'"

Amber was studying integers in her math class and thought she could use these ideas of "in the black" and "in the red" to model the addition of positive and negative integers. Her model uses a chip board and black and red chips. Each black chip represents $^+1$, and each red chip represents $^-1$.

For example, this chip board shows a value of $^+5$:

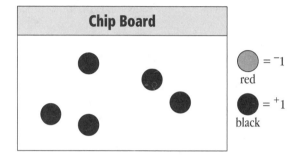

This chip board shows a value of $^-5$:

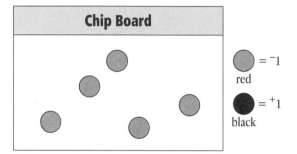

To represent $^-4 + {}^-3$, Amber started with an empty chip board. She represented $^-4$ by putting four red chips on the board.

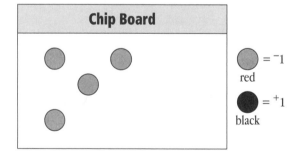

To represent the addition of ⁻3, she put three more red chips on the board.

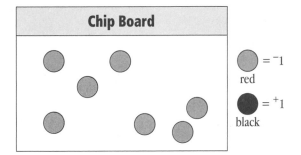

Since there were seven red chips on the board, Amber concluded that the sum of ⁻4 and ⁻3 is ⁻7. She wrote the number sentence ⁻4 + ⁻3 = ⁻7 to represent what she did on the chip board.

Amber showed her idea to her friend Adil. Adil liked Amber's model, but he wasn't sure how to use it to add a negative integer and a positive integer. Amber explained by modeling ⁻4 + ⁺5. She started by clearing the board. She then put four red chips on the board to represent ⁻4.

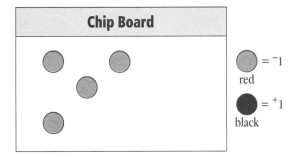

To add ⁺5, Amber added five black chips to the board.

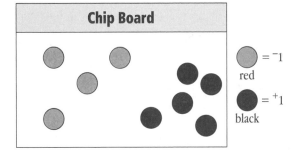

Amber said that next she had to simplify the board so that the answer would be easier to read. She reminded Adil that since $^+1$ and $^-1$ are opposites, they add to 0. So, a pair consisting of one black chip ($^+1$) and one red chip ($^-1$) represents 0. Amber formed as many black-red pairs as she could.

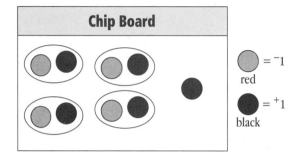

Since each black-red pair represents 0, all the black-red pairs can be removed from the board without changing the total value on the board. After Amber removed these "zeros" from the board, only one black chip remained, representing a sum of $^+1$.

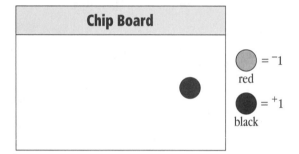

Adil wrote $^-4 + {}^+5 = {}^+1$ to represent the problem Amber had modeled.

Problem 2.2

A. Use a chip board and black and red chips to find each sum. Draw a series of chip boards to illustrate your work.

   1. $^-8 + {}^-7$ **2.** $^-8 + {}^+7$ **3.** $^+8 + {}^-7$ **4.** $^+8 + {}^+7$

B. Find two combinations of black and red chips that will simplify to represent the given integer. Draw a series of chip boards to prove that each combination works.

   1. $^-3$ **2.** $^+5$

C. Write each combination you found in part B as an addition sentence.

■ Problem 2.2 Follow-Up

1. What integer added to $^-8$ gives a sum of $^-4$?

2. Give two integers with a sum that is less than either of the two integers.

3. Give two integers with a sum that is greater than either of the two integers.

Conrado was adding the integers $^-5$ and $^+8$ on a chip board. First, he represented $^-5$ and $^+8$.

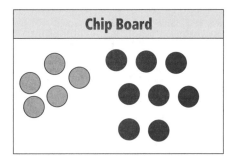

He then rearranged the chips to form a group of five red chips (representing $^-5$) and a group of five black chips (representing $^+5$). Since the two groups add to 0, he removed them from the board.

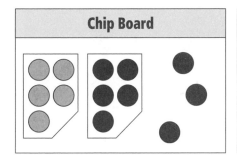 

He wrote a series of equations to represent what he had done on the chip board.

$$^-5 + {^+8} = {^-5} + {^+5} + {^+3}$$
$$= ({^-5} + {^+5}) + {^+3}$$
$$= 0 + {^+3}$$
$$= {^+3}$$

Conrado thought that this method of regrouping to find numbers with a sum of 0 would be a good way to compute sums in his head.

4. Use Conrado's method to compute the following sums in your head.
   a. $^+9 + {^-7}$ **b.** $^-80 + {^+50}$ **c.** $^+35 + {^-27}$ **d.** $^-8 + {^-5}$

As you work on these ACE questions, use your calculator whenever you need it.

Applications

In 1–3, illustrate the addition problem on a number line, and give the answer.

1. $6 + {}^-6$

2. ${}^-4 + {}^-3 + {}^-8$

3. ${}^+8 + {}^-11 + {}^-9$

In 4–7, write the addition sentence illustrated by the figure.

4.

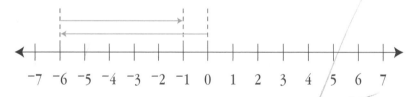

5.

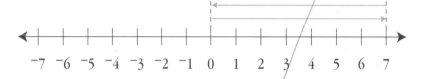

6.

7.

In 8 and 9, use the chip board below.

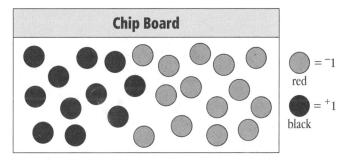

Chip Board

= ⁻1
red

= ⁺1
black

8. **a.** After you simplify the board by removing zeros (black-red pairs), what chips would remain? What integer do these chips represent?

    b. Give another combination of black and red chips that would simplify to give the same result you got in part a.

9. Starting with the board as shown above, the following series of actions takes place. Write an addition sentence to describe each action. (A correct addition sentence will show the previous value represented by the board, the value of the chips that are added, and the new value represented by the board.)

    a. Seven black chips are added.

    b. Three more black chips are added.

    c. Three red chips are added.

10. **a.** Find two combinations of black and red chips that simplify to represent ⁻11.

    b. Draw a chip board to represent each combination from part a.

    c. Write an addition sentence to represent each combination from part a.

11. **a.** Find two combinations of black and red chips that simplify to represent ⁺7.

    b. Draw a chip board to represent each combination from part a.

    c. Write an addition sentence to represent each combination from part a.

In 12 and 13, use the chip board shown below.

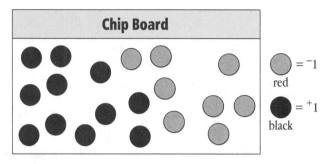

Chip Board

○ = ⁻1
red

● = ⁺1
black

12. After you simplify the board by removing zeros (black-red pairs), what chips would remain? What integer do these chips represent?

13. Starting with the board as shown above, the following series of actions takes place. Write an addition sentence to describe each action. (A correct addition sentence will show the previous value represented by the board, the value of the chips that are added, and the new value represented by the board.)

    a. Four black chips are added.

    b. Ten red chips are added.

    c. Six black chips are added.

    d. Eight more black chips are added.

    e. Eight red chips are added.

In 14–17, illustrate the addition problem on a number line or a series of chip boards, and give the answer.

14. ⁺12 + ⁻4   **15.** ⁻5 + ⁺5

16. ⁺5 + ⁻9   **17.** ⁻3 + ⁻6

In 18–26, find the sum.

18. ⁻105 + ⁺65   **19.** ⁺1050 + ⁻150   **20.** ⁻99 + ⁻47

21. ⁺37 + ⁻12 + ⁻15   **22.** 0 + ⁻400   **23.** ⁻120 + ⁻225

24. ⁻90 + ⁻90   **25.** ⁻90 + 0   **26.** ⁺35 + ⁻35

In 27 and 28, decide whether the statement is always true, sometimes true, or always false. Give examples to illustrate your answer.

27. The sum of two negative integers is a negative integer.

28. The sum of a negative integer and a positive integer is a positive integer.

Connections

29. In Duluth, Minnesota, the temperature at 6:00 A.M. on January 1 was $^{-}30°$F. During the next 8 hours, the temperature rose 38°. Then, during the next 12 hours, the temperature dropped 12°. Finally, in the next 4 hours, it rose 15°. What was the temperature at 6:00 A.M. on January 2?

30. Most businesses try hard to make a profit. However, new businesses usually have start-up costs that put them "in the hole" at first. Suppose your family decides to open a bike shop. To get started, you'll have to make a down payment on the rent for your shop, buy bicycles and other supplies to stock the shop, and invest in business equipment and paper to keep track of income and expenses.

Below is a series of business transactions for the bike shop. For each transaction, write an addition sentence that shows how the new balance is calculated from the old balance.

a. Down payment of two months' shop rent: $1800

b. Payment for 20 new bicycles: $2150

c. Down payment of rent on office equipment: $675

d. Business insurance for 6 months: $2300

e. Sale of three bicycles: $665

f. Sale of two helmets and one baby seat: $95

g. Advertising in the yellow pages: $250

h. Sale of six bicycles: $1150

i. Refund for unhappy customer: $225

j. Sale of two bicycles, two helmets, and two air pumps: $750

k. Refund from return of five bicycles to manufacturer: $530

Extensions

31. **a.** Which integers, when added to ⁻15, give a sum greater than 0?

b. Which integers, when added to ⁻15, give a sum less than 0?

c. Which integers, when added to ⁻15, give a sum of 0?

32. A chip board starts out with five black chips. Chips are added to the board. After the board is simplified by removing zeros (black-red pairs), nine black chips remain.

a. What chips might have been added? Give two possibilities. (For example, adding five black chips and one red chip results in ten black chips and one red chip. After you remove zeros, nine black chips remain.)

b. Write an addition sentence for each of the possibilities you gave in part a. (For the example given in part a, the addition sentence would be ⁺5 + ⁺5 + ⁻1 = ⁺9).

33. A chip board starts out empty. Chips are added to the board. After the board is simplified by removing zeros (black-red pairs), one black chip remains.

a. What chips might have been added? Give two possibilities.

b. Write an addition sentence for each of the possibilities you gave in part a.

34. A chip board starts out with one black chip. Chips are added to the board. After the board is simplified by removing zeros (black-red pairs), five red chips remain.

a. What chips might have been added? Give two possibilities.

b. Write an addition sentence for each of the possibilities you gave in part a.

35. A chip board starts out with five red chips. Chips are added to the board. After the board is simplified by removing zeros (black-red pairs), eight red chips remain.

a. What chips might have been added? Give two possibilities.

b. Write an addition sentence for each of the possibilities you gave in part a.

36. A chip board starts out empty. Chips are added to the board. After the board is simplified by removing zeros (black-red pairs), two red chips remain.

   a. What chips might have been added? Give two possibilities.

   b. Write an addition sentence for each of the possibilities you gave in part a.

37. A chip board starts out with two red chips. Chips are added to the board. After the board is simplified by removing zeros (black-red pairs), five black chips remain.

   a. What chips might have been added? Give two possibilities.

   b. Write an addition sentence for each of the possibilities you gave in part a.

Mathematical Reflections

In this investigation, you explored two ways to model the addition of integers—on a number line and with a chip board. These questions will help you summarize what you have learned:

1 When you add two integers, how can you decide whether their sum will be positive, negative, or zero?

2 Describe how to add any two integers.

3 Explain how you can find the opposite of a number. Use the following examples to illustrate your explanations.

   a. 7   **b.** 0   **c.** $^-12$

Think about your answers to these questions, discuss your ideas with other students and your teacher, and then write a summary of your findings in your journal.

Subtracting Integers

In the last investigation, you used number lines and chip boards to help you learn about the addition of integers. These tools are also helpful for modeling subtraction of integers. In this investigation, you will start by using a chip board to explore subtraction. Next, you will use the relationship between addition and subtraction to subtract numbers on the number line. Finally, you will study patterns involving subtraction of integers and use these patterns to make predictions.

Think about this!

You can use positive and negative numbers to describe elevations. If you think of sea level as 0 feet, you can express elevations above sea level with positive numbers and elevations below sea level with negative numbers.

The highest point in the United States is Mount McKinley (also known as Denali), Alaska, with an elevation of 20,320 feet above sea level. You can express this elevation as $^+20{,}320$ feet. The lowest point in the United States is Death Valley, California, with an elevation of 282 feet below sea level. You can express this elevation as $^-282$ feet.

Death Valley, California

How many feet higher is the highest point in the United States than the lowest point?

3.1 Subtracting on a Chip Board

Amber's friends Jing-mei and Drew liked Amber's chip board model for adding integers. They decided to use a chip board to explore subtracting integers.

To model 9 − 5, Jing-mei started with an empty chip board and then put nine black chips on the board to represent ⁺9.

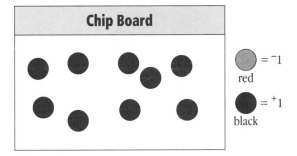

Jing-mei thinks about subtracting as "taking away." Therefore, to represent subtracting 5, she *removed* five black chips from the board.

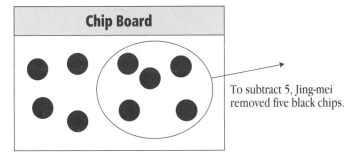

To subtract 5, Jing-mei removed five black chips.

After removing the five black chips, four black chips remained.

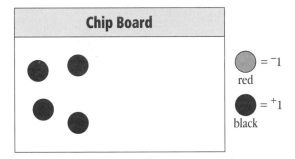

Jing-mei wrote the number sentence 9 − 5 = 4 to represent her work on the chip board.

Drew tried Jing-mei's method to find ⁻11 – ⁻5. He started with an empty board and then put on 11 red chips to represent ⁻11.

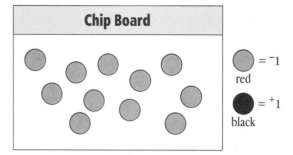

Like Jing-mei, Drew thought of subtracting as "taking away." To represent subtracting ⁻5, he removed five red chips from the board.

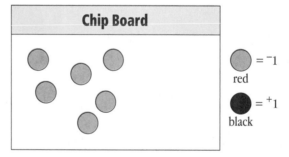

To subtract ⁻5, Drew removed five red chips.

Six red chips remained on the board.

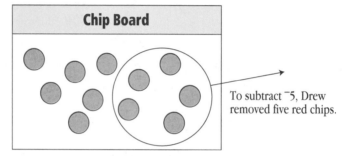

Drew wrote the number sentence ⁻11 – ⁻5 = ⁻6 to represent his work on the chip board.

Think about this!

Why does it makes sense that the difference between 9 and 5 is 4 (that is, 9 – 5 = 4) and the difference between ⁻11 and ⁻5 is ⁻6 (that is, ⁻11 – ⁻5 = ⁻6)?

A. Use a chip board and black and red chips to find each sum or difference.

    1. ⁻8 – ⁻7   **2.** ⁺8 + ⁻7

    3. ⁻6 – ⁻2   **4.** ⁺6 + ⁻2

B. In Problem 2.2, you simplified chip boards to find the number represented. For example, each chip board below represents ⁺3.

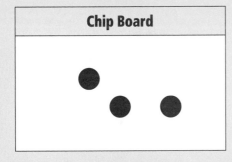
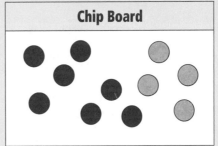

    Find three ways to represent ⁻8 on a chip board.

C. Jing-mei wants to find ⁻8 – ⁻10 by using a chip board. She puts eight red chips on the board to represent ⁻8 but then gets stuck because she cannot remove ten red chips to represent subtracting ⁻10.

    How can Jing-mei show ⁻8 on a chip board so that she can remove ten red chips? What is ⁻8 – ⁻10? Explain how you determined your answer.

D. Drew wants to find ⁺5 – ⁺7 by using a chip board. How can he show ⁺5 on a chip board so that he can remove seven black chips to represent subtracting ⁺7? What is ⁺5 – ⁺7? Explain how you determined your answer.

E. Use a chip board and black and red chips to find each difference. For each difference, tell how many chips of each color you used to represent the first integer so that you could take away chips to represent subtracting the second integer.

    1. 10 – 12   **2.** 7 – ⁻2

    3. ⁻5 – 6   **4.** ⁻3 – ⁻7

To find ⁺5 − ⁺7, Drew started by showing ⁺5 as five black chips.

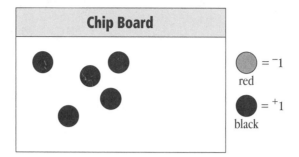

He could not represent subtracting ⁺7 because there were not seven black chips to remove from the board.

He recalled that adding or removing a black-red pair does not change the value of the board because such a pair represents 0 (⁺1 and ⁻1 are opposites, so they combine to 0). He added a black-red pair to the board.

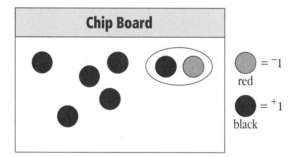

The board now had six black chips and one red chip. To subtract ⁺7, Drew needed to remove seven black chips, so he added one more black-red pair.

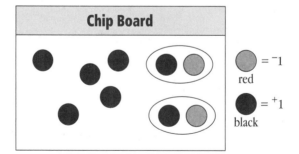

Then Drew was able to represent the subtraction. He removed seven black chips from the board. Two red chips remained.

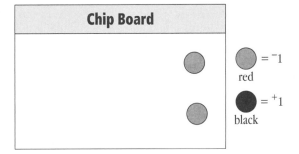

Chip Board

red = $^-1$

black = $^+1$

Drew wrote the number sentence $^+5 - {}^+7 = {}^-2$ to represent his work on the chip board.

1. Find three ways to show $^-5$ on the chip board. For each representation, write a subtraction problem that would be easy to solve if you started with that representation.

You have seen that there are lots of ways to represent a given integer on a chip board. For example, you could represent $^+5$ with eight black chips and three red chips or with six black chips and one red chip. However, there is only one way to represent a given integer with only one color. For example, the only way to represent $^+5$ with one color is by using five black chips, and the only way to represent $^-5$ with one color is by using five red chips.

The number of chips needed to represent an integer *with only one color* is the **absolute value** of the integer. Thus, the absolute value of 5 is 5, and the absolute value of $^-5$ is 5. We represent the absolute value of a number by writing a straight, vertical line segment on each side of the number. The equation $|^-5| = 5$ is read, "The absolute value of negative five equals five."

2. Find each absolute value.
  a. $|^-7|$ **b.** $|18|$ **c.** $|^-42|$ **d.** $|0|$

3. Tell which numbers have the given number as their absolute value.
  a. 12   **b.** 3   **c.** 31   **d.** 100

3.2 Subtracting on a Number Line

When you add integers by using a chip board, you add chips to the board. When you subtract integers, you remove chips from the board. Just as you can think of adding and removing chips as opposite "moves," you can think of adding and subtracting integers as opposite, or *inverse*, operations. This idea can help you understand how subtraction is modeled on a number line.

opposites attract

To model the *addition* sentence $^+7 + ^+5 = ^+12$ on a number line, you start at 0 and move 7 units to the right to represent $^+7$.

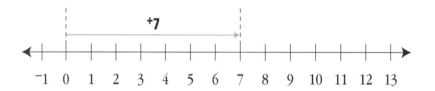

To *add* $^+5$, you move 5 more units to the *right*.

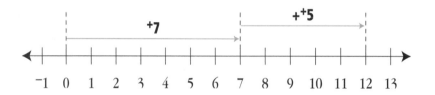

To model the *subtraction* sentence $^+7 - ^+5 = ^+2$, you can use the idea of opposite operations. Start at 0, and then move 7 units to the right to represent $^+7$.

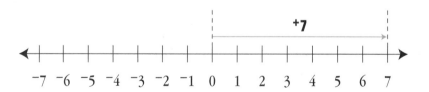

To *subtract* $^+5$, move to the *left*—opposite the direction you moved to add $^+5$.

In other words, since subtraction is the opposite of addition, you subtract a number on the number line by moving in the opposite direction you would to add the number.

Let's use this idea to find $^-11 - ^-5$. First, start at 0, and move 11 units to the left to represent $^-11$.

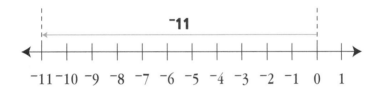

Next, you must subtract $^-5$. To add $^-5$, you would move 5 units to the left, so to subtract $^-5$, you must move 5 units to the right. You end at $^-6$.

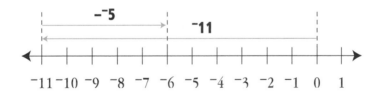

You can write the number sentence $^-11 - ^-5 = ^-6$ to represent your work on the number line.

Notice in the example above that *subtracting* $^-5$ is the same as *adding* $^+5$.

Problem 3.2

A. Use a number line to find each difference. Use a chip board to check your work.

1. $^+7 - {}^+9$ **2.** $^-7 - {}^+9$ **3.** $^+7 - {}^-9$ **4.** $^-7 - {}^-9$

B. Use a number line to find each sum or difference.

1. $^+12 - {}^+3$ **2.** $^+12 + {}^-3$ **3.** $^-10 - {}^-7$ **4.** $^-10 + {}^+7$

C. Find the distance between each pair of numbers on a number line. In each case, tell how the distance is related to the difference between the two numbers.

1. 1 and 5   **2.** $^-1$ and 5   **3.** $^-5$ and $^-9$ **4.** $^-3$ and 3

D. Write two number sentences illustrated by this figure.

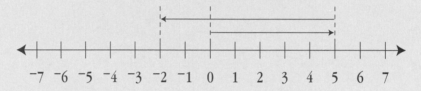

Problem 3.2 Follow-Up

1. When you add two positive integers, you get a positive sum. When you subtract two positive integers, do you always get a positive difference? Explain.

2. When you use the number line model, you can think of the *absolute value* of a number as its distance from 0. For example, 3 and $^-3$ are each 3 units from 0, so the absolute value of each number is 3.

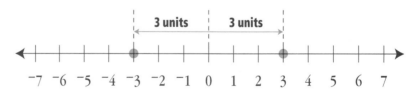

Use a number line to help you find a pair of numbers with the given absolute value.

a. 10   **b.** 5   **c.** 1   **d.** 7

Exploring Patterns

Studying and describing patterns are an important part of mathematics. Study the patterns in the equations below, and then work on the problem.

$$15 - 5 = 10$$
$$15 - 4 = 11$$
$$15 - 3 = 12$$
$$15 - 2 = 13$$
$$15 - 1 = 14$$
$$15 - 0 = 15$$

Problem 3.3

A. Describe any patterns you observe in the way the differences change as the integers subtracted from 15 get smaller.

B. Use the patterns you observed to predict the answer to $15 - {}^-1$. Check your prediction by using a chip board or number line.

C. Predict the answer to $15 - {}^-4$. Explain your reasoning.

■ Problem 3.3 Follow-Up

1. Study the equations below.

$$^-10 - 5 = {}^-15$$
$$^-10 - 4 = {}^-14$$
$$^-10 - 3 = {}^-13$$
$$^-10 - 2 = {}^-12$$
$$^-10 - 1 = {}^-11$$
$$^-10 - 0 = {}^-10$$

a. Describe any patterns you observe in the way the differences change as the integers subtracted from $^-10$ get smaller.

b. Use the patterns you observed to predict the answer to $^-10 - {}^-1$. Check your answer by using a chip board or number line.

c. Predict the answer to $^-10 - {}^-6$. Explain your reasoning.

2. When you add two negative integers, you get a negative sum. When you subtract two negative integers, do you always get a negative difference? Explain.

3.4 "Undoing" with Addition and Subtraction

You can use the chip boards below to think about the addition sentence $11 + 3 = 14$. The chip board on the left shows 11 black chips. On the chip board on the right, 3 more black chips have been added for a total of 14 black chips.

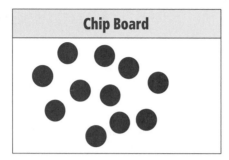

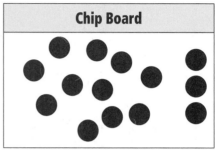

If you removed 3 black chips from the 14 black chips on the second board, you would end up with 11 chips, as you had on the starting board. In other words, removing chips from the board "undoes" placing chips on the board. You can represent this "undoing" with the subtraction sentence $11 = 14 - 3$. So, just as you can think of removing 3 chips from the board as "undoing" placing 3 chips on the board, you can think of the subtraction sentence $11 = 14 - 3$ as "undoing" the addition sentence $11 + 3 = 14$.

You can use this idea of undoing addition to find a subtraction sentence for a given addition sentence.

Problem 3.4

A. 1. Complete the addition sentence $^-17 + 13 = ?$.

    2. Write a subtraction sentence that "undoes" the addition sentence you found in part 1.

B. 1. Complete the addition sentence $^-4 + ^-18 = ?$.

    2. Write a subtraction sentence that "undoes" the addition sentence you found in part 1.

C. Write a subtraction sentence that solves each problem.

    1. $? + ^-18 = 6$ **2.** $? + ^-13 = ^-41$

    3. $? + 6.1 = ^-3.2$ **4.** $? + ^-\frac{1}{3} = \frac{1}{3}$

D. Write an addition sentence that solves each problem.

    1. $? - ^-6 = ^-6$ **2.** $? - ^-2 = 3$

    3. $? - 5.3 = ^-7.1$ **4.** $? - ^-\frac{1}{4} = ^-\frac{3}{4}$

Problem 3.4 Follow–Up

1. In the introduction to this problem, we wrote the number sentence $11 = 14 - 3$ from the sentence $11 + 3 = 14$. We could also write $3 + 11 = 14$. Can you write a different subtraction sentence to go with this addition sentence?

2. a. Complete the addition sentence $3.8 + {}^-2.6 = ?$.

   b. Write all the subtraction sentences you can that are related to the addition sentence you found in part a.

3. a. Complete the subtraction sentence ${}^-11 - 6 = ?$.

   b. Write all the addition sentences you can that are related to the subtraction sentence you found in part a.

4. When you add positive and negative integers, sometimes you get a positive sum and sometimes you get a negative sum. Is the same true when you subtract positive and negative integers? Explain.

As you work on these ACE questions, use your calculator whenever you need it.

Applications

1. When the finance committee for the Westover School Dance met on October 22, they had a balance of $50.25 in their checking account. Since then, the following transactions have taken place. Find the balance in the checking account after each transaction.

a. The committee deposited $44 they received from ticket sales.

b. Two students asked for refunds for their tickets. These tickets were worth a total of $8. The committee treasurer wrote these students checks for their refunds.

c. The finance committee got a $25 refund from the bakery because the refreshments committee decided to bake their own cookies and cakes. They deposited the refund into the checking account.

d. The committee gave the school principal $50 to pay the custodian who would open, clean, and close the school on the night of the party.

e. The DJ called to say she couldn't work at the party because her sound system was broken. She returned the committee's $50 deposit, which they deposited into the checking account.

In 2–10, find the sum or difference. Be prepared to explain how you got your answer.

2. $^+12 + {}^+4$ **3.** $^+5 - {}^+9$ **4.** $^+5 + {}^-9$

5. $^-3 - {}^+6$ **6.** $^-3 + {}^-6$ **7.** $^+7 - {}^-5$

8. $^+7 - {}^+5$ **9.** $^-7 - {}^-5$ **10.** $^+3.8 - {}^-4.2$

11. Write an addition sentence to describe this chip board.

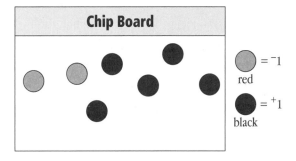

In 12–14, draw chip boards to help you find the difference.

12. $3 - 5$ **13.** $5 - 3$ **14.** $3 - {}^-2$

In 15 and 16, write an addition sentence and a subtraction sentence to represent what is shown on the number line.

15.

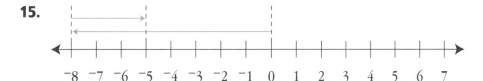

16.

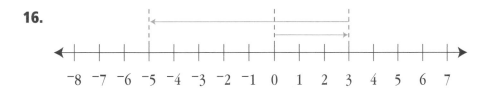

In 17–20, find the distance between the two numbers on the number line.

17. 9 and 4   **18.** $^-9$ and 4   **19.** $^-9$ and $^-4$ **20.** 0 and $^-7$

In 21 and 22, refer to the chip board below.

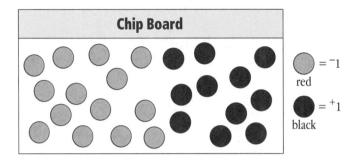

21. After you simplify the board by removing zeros (black-red pairs), what chips would remain? What integer do these chips represent?

22. Starting with the board as shown above, the following series of actions takes place. Write a number sentence to describe each action.

    a. Nine black chips are added.

    b. Seven black chips are removed.

    c. Four red chips are removed.

    d. Three black chips are removed.

In 23 and 24, refer to the chip board below. Each black chip represents $1, and each red chip represents ⁻$1.

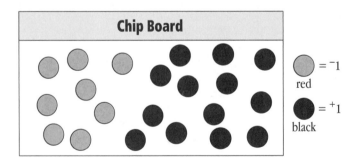

23. What "balance" is shown on this board?

24. Starting with the board as shown on the previous page, the following series of "transactions" takes place. Find the new balance after each transaction.

   a. Four black chips are added.

   b. Ten red chips are added.

   c. Six black chips are added.

   d. Eight black chips are removed.

   e. Five red chips are removed.

In 25 and 26, decide whether the statement is always true, sometimes true, or always false. Give examples to illustrate your thinking.

25. If a negative integer is subtracted from a positive integer, the difference is a negative integer.

26. If a negative integer is subtracted from a negative integer, the difference is a negative integer.

In 27–32, find the sum or difference.

27. $^-756 + 398$

28. $^-756 + ^-398$

29. $3138 + ^-2149$

30. $3138 - ^-2149$

31. $3138 - 5149$

32. $^-3138 - 5149$

33. **a.** Name all integers that have an absolute value of 12.

   b. Name all integers that are 12 units from 0 on the number line.

   c. Name all integers that are 12 units from $^-8$ on the number line.

   d. Write two subtraction problems that relate to your answer in part c.

Connections

34. Records at Jefferson Hospital showed the following information about the number of patients received and discharged:

Day 1: received 12 patients and discharged 9 patients
Day 2: received 14 patients and discharged 21 patients
Day 3: received 5 patients and discharged 14 patients
Day 4: received 11 patients and discharged 10 patients

How did the number of patients in the hospital at the end of the four-day period compare with the number of patients at the start of the four-day period?

35. Write three addition problems that have ⁻7 as a sum.

36. Write three addition problems that have 12 as a sum.

37. Write three subtraction problems that have ⁻7 as a difference.

38. Write three subtraction problems that have 12 as a difference.

Extensions

39. Juan said that he had discovered a new method for subtracting integers. He gave this example to illustrate his method:

$$^+7 - {}^+9 = {}^+7 - (^+7 + {}^+2) = (^+7 - {}^+7) - {}^+2 = 0 - {}^+2 = {}^-2$$

a. Is Juan's method correct? Draw chip boards to explain your answer.

b. Explain Juan's method in words.

40. On many scientific calculators, you use the $\boxed{+/-}$ or $\boxed{(-)}$ key to enter a negative number. This means that evaluating problems with lots of negative numbers like the ones below requires many keystrokes. For each problem below, find an equivalent problem that you could enter into a calculator to avoid using the $\boxed{+/-}$ or $\boxed{(-)}$ key as much as possible.

a. $^-12 - {}^-7 - {}^-9 - {}^-10 - {}^-4$

b. $^-12 - 7 - {}^-9 + 10 - {}^-4 + 13 + {}^-20$

Mathematical Reflections

In this investigation, you explored situations that involve subtraction of integers. You explored subtraction by using chip boards and number lines and by looking at patterns. These questions will help you summarize what you have learned:

1 Write a strategy for finding the difference of two integers. Be sure to consider all possible combinations of positive integers, negative integers, and 0. Verify your strategy by finding the following differences.

   a. $5 - 9$ **b.** $^-5 - {}^+3$ **c.** $^-5 - {}^-3$ **d.** $5 - {}^-9$

2 Without actually calculating the sum, how can you decide if the sum of two integers is positive? Negative? Zero?

3 Without actually calculating the difference, how can you decide if the difference of two integers is positive? Negative? Zero?

4 Describe how addition and subtraction of integers are related.

5 Describe how to find the absolute value of any number.

Think about your answers to these questions, discuss your ideas with other students and your teacher, and then write a summary of your findings in your journal.

Multiplying and Dividing Integers

In the previous investigations, you looked at various ways to think about and model addition and subtraction of integers. In this investigation, you will explore ways to think about multiplying and dividing integers.

4.1 Rising and Falling Temperatures

In Investigation 1, you used a thermometer to explore positive and negative numbers. In this problem, you will use a thermometer to help you think about multiplying integers.

In this investigation, we will use a positive symbol to represent a rise in temperature and a negative symbol to represent a drop in temperature. That means, for example, if the temperature rises 3°, we will say that it changes by $^+3°$, and if the temperature drops 3°, we will say that it changes by $^-3°$.

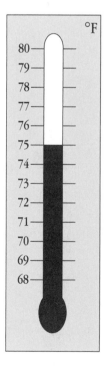 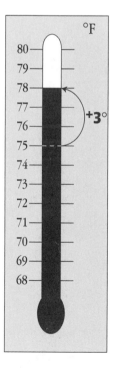 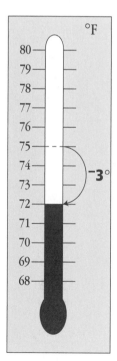

Problem 4.1

A. 1. Suppose the temperature changed by an average of $^+3°$ per hour for a 10-hour period. Copy and complete the table below, and use it to find the total temperature change for the first 5 hours.

Number of hours	1	2	3	4	5
Total temperature change	$^+3°$	$^+6°$			

2. Write a multiplication sentence that represents the total change in temperature for the first 5 hours. Write a multiplication sentence that represents the total change in temperature for the entire 10-hour period.

B. 1. Suppose the temperature changed by an average of $^-3°$ per hour for a 10-hour period. Copy and complete the table below, and use it to find the total temperature change for the first 5 hours.

Number of hours	1	2	3	4	5
Total temperature change	$^-3°$	$^-6°$			

2. Write a multiplication sentence that represents the total change in temperature for the first 5 hours. Write a multiplication sentence that represents the total change in temperature for the entire 10-hour period.

C. 1. Write the addition sentence illustrated by each diagram below.

2. Write the multiplication sentence illustrated by each diagram below.

a.
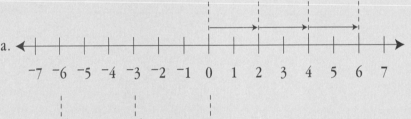

b.
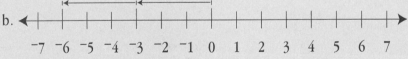

c.
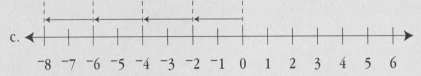

D. Make up a situation about temperatures that can be expressed as $4 \times {}^-10$.

E. Find each product.

1. $5 \times {}^-4$ **2.** $20 \times {}^-4$ **3.** $^-4 \times 20$ **4.** $^-5 \times 4$

1. Suppose the temperature changed by an average of $^+2°$ per hour from its low of $^-4°$F at 3:00 A.M. What was the temperature at 1:00 P.M.?

2. Suppose the temperature changed by an average of $^-1.5°$ per hour from its high of $^+25°$F at noon. What was the temperature at 10:00 P.M.?

3. When you add a positive integer and a negative integer, you sometimes get a positive result and sometimes get a negative result. Is the same true when you multiply a positive integer and a negative integer? Explain.

Did you know?

The temperature at the center of the Sun is estimated to be about 15,000,000°C. The temperature at the center of a thermonuclear fusion bomb is about 400,000,000°C! Temperature does not appear to have an upper limit. However, there does seem to be a lower limit. Scientists believe that $^-273.15°$C, a temperature known as *absolute zero*, is the lowest temperature attainable. At this temperature the molecules and atoms of a substance have the least possible energy.

4.2 Studying Multiplication Patterns

In Investigation 3, you studied patterns to help you understand subtraction of integers. Studying patterns can also help you think about multiplication of integers. Study the equations below, and then work on the problem.

$$5 \times 5 = 25$$
$$5 \times 4 = 20$$
$$5 \times 3 = 15$$
$$5 \times 2 = 10$$
$$5 \times 1 = 5$$
$$5 \times 0 = 0$$

Problem 4.2

A. Describe any patterns you observe in the way the products change as the integers multiplied by 5 get smaller.

B. 1. Use the patterns you observed to predict $5 \times {}^-1$. Explain your reasoning.

2. Write the next four equations in the pattern.

C. Complete the equations below, and use them to help you answer parts D and E.

$$5 \times {}^-4 = ?$$
$$4 \times {}^-4 = ?$$
$$3 \times {}^-4 = ?$$
$$2 \times {}^-4 = ?$$
$$1 \times {}^-4 = ?$$
$$0 \times {}^-4 = ?$$

D. Describe any patterns you observe in the way the products change as the integers multiplied by $^-4$ get smaller.

E. 1. Use the patterns you observed to predict $^-1 \times {}^-4$. Explain your reasoning.

2. Write the next four equations in the pattern.

F. Find the following products.

1. $^-3 \times 7$ **2.** $5 \times {}^-8$ **3.** $^-11 \times {}^-12$ **4.** $^-3.6 \times 2.7$

Problem 4.2 Follow-Up

1. a. Find $^-6 \times 7$ and $7 \times ^-6$.

  b. When you multiply integers, does the order of the numbers matter?

2. a. Find $^-6 + 7$ and $7 + ^-6$.

  b. When you add integers, does the order of the numbers matter?

3. a. Find $^-6 - 7$ and $7 - ^-6$.

  b. When you subtract integers, does the order of the numbers matter?

4. When you add two negative integers, you get a negative result. Is the same true when you multiply two negative integers? Explain.

4.3 Playing the Integer Product Game

In this problem, you will practice multiplying integers by playing the Integer Product Game. The Integer Product Game board consists of a list of factors and a grid of products. Two players compete to get four squares in a row—up and down, across, or diagonally. To play the game, you will need Labsheet 4.3, two paper clips, and colored markers or game chips. The rules for the game and the game board are given on the next page.

> **Problem 4.3**
>
> Play the game with a partner. Look for interesting patterns and ideas that might help you devise a winning strategy. Make notes of your observations.

Problem 4.3 Follow-Up

1. Give every combination of two factors from the factor list that will give each of the following products.

  a. 5   **b.** $^-12$ **c.** 12   **d.** $^-25$

2. Your opponent starts the game by putting a paper clip on $^-4$. What products are possible on your turn?

3. At the end of your opponent's turn, the paper clips are on $^-5$ and $^-2$. What move would you make to get a product of $^-15$?

4. At the end of your opponent's turn, the paper clips are on $^-3$ and $^-2$. What move would you make to get a product of $^-6$?

5. Why doesn't $^-35$ appear on the board?

Integer Product Game Rules

1. Player A puts a paper clip on a number in the factor list. Player A does not cover a square on the product grid because only one factor has been marked; it takes two factors to make a product.

2. Player B puts the other paper clip on any number in the factor list (including the same number marked by Player A) and then shades or covers the product of the two factors on the product grid.

3. Player A moves *either one* of the paper clips to another number and then shades or covers the new product using a different color from Player B.

4. Each player, in turn, moves a paper clip and marks a product. If a product is already marked, the player does not get a mark for that turn. The winner is the first player to mark four squares in a row—up and down, across, or diagonally.

The Integer Product Game

1	‾1	2	‾2	3	‾3
4	‾4	5	‾5	6	‾6
8	‾8	9	‾9	10	‾10
12	‾12	15	‾15	16	‾16
18	‾18	20	‾20	24	‾24
25	‾25	30	‾30	36	‾36

Factors:
‾6 ‾5 ‾4 ‾3 ‾2 ‾1 1 2 3 4 5 6

4.4 Dividing Integers

In Investigation 3, you saw that subtraction is the opposite, or inverse, of addition. You observed that for any addition sentence, you can write a subtraction sentence that undoes the addition. Similarly, division is the opposite, or inverse, of multiplication, and for any multiplication sentence, you can write a division sentence that undoes the multiplication.

For example, given the multiplication sentence $5 \times 6 = 30$, you can write two division sentences:

$$5 = 30 \div 6 \text{ and } 6 = 30 \div 5$$

Problem 4.4

A. 1. Complete the multiplication sentence $^-5 \times 6 = ?$.
   2. Write two division sentences that are equivalent to the multiplication sentence you found in part 1.

B. 1. Complete the multiplication sentence $^-8 \times {}^-4 = ?$.
   2. Write two division sentences that are equivalent to the multiplication sentence you found in part 1.

C. Write a division sentence that solves each problem.
   1. $? \times 12 = {}^-132$ **2.** $^-8 \times ? = {}^-56$
   3. $? \times {}^-4 = 132$ **4.** $5.2 \times ? = {}^-8.84$

D. Write a division or a multiplication sentence that solves each problem.
   1. $? \div {}^-3 = {}^-8$ **2.** $91 \div ? = {}^-7$
   3. $? \div 11 = {}^-17$ **4.** $^-19.95 \div ? = 9.5$

Problem 4.4 Follow-Up

1. Find each quotient.
   a. $^-121 \div 11$ **b.** $121 \div {}^-11$ **c.** $^-96 \div {}^-4$ **d.** $96 \div 4$

2. a. Find $18 \div 3$.
   b. How does your answer from part a help you find $^-18 \div 3$, $18 \div {}^-3$, and $^-18 \div {}^-3$?

As you work on these ACE questions, use your calculator whenever you need it.

Applications

1. On Tuesday, a cold front passed through, causing the temperature to change ⁻2°F per hour from noon until 10:00 A.M. the next morning. The temperature at noon on Tuesday was 75°F.

   a. What was the temperature at 4:00 P.M. Tuesday?

   b. What was the temperature at 9:00 A.M. Wednesday?

2. **a.** Write the addition sentence illustrated by the number line below.

   b. Write the multiplication sentence illustrated by the number line below.

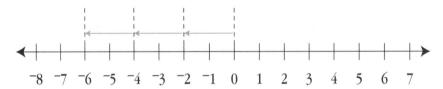

3. **a.** Write the addition sentence illustrated by the number line below.

   b. Write the multiplication sentence illustrated by the number line below.

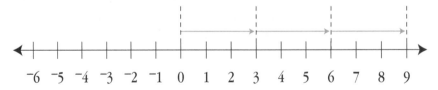

In 4–7, list all the integer factor pairs for the number.

4. 11   **5.** ⁻21   **6.** 12   **7.** ⁻12

8. Iseku and Kylie are making a version of the Integer Product Game in which players need three products in a row to win. What factors do they need for their game?

Iseku and Kylie's Product Game

4	⁻4	6	⁻6
9	⁻9	10	⁻10
15	⁻15	25	⁻25

In 9–16, find the sum, difference, product, or quotient.

9. 52×75 10. $52 \times {}^-75$ 11. $2262 \div 58$ 12. $10{,}680 \div {}^-120$

13. $137 + 899$ 14. $5679 - 7890$ 15. ${}^-4329 - {}^-1234$ 16. ${}^-9908 \div {}^-89$

Connections

In 17–21, write a number sentence to represent the situation described. Then tell whether more than one number sentence is possible, and explain your reasoning.

17. The temperature at noon was ⁻13°C. For the next 6 hours, the temperature changed by an average of ⁺1.8° per hour. What was the temperature at 6:00 P.M.?

18. The temperature at noon was ⁻13°C. From 6:00 A.M. until noon, the temperature had changed by an average of ⁺5° per hour. What had the temperature been at 6:00 A.M.?

19. In a game of MathMania, the Extraterrestrials had a score of ⁻300, and then they answered four 50-point questions incorrectly. What was their score after missing the four questions?

20. After answering three 100-point questions correctly, the Supermutants had 200 points. What was their score before answering the three questions?

21. The Bigtown Bears were on their own 25-yard line. For the next three plays, they lost an average of 4 yards per play. Where did the Bears end up after the three plays?

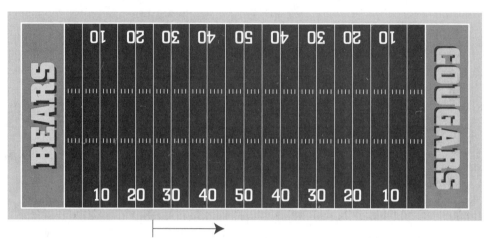

The Bears are here now and are moving from left to right—
that is, they move right when they gain yards.

In 22–25, complete the number sentence, and then write an equivalent sentence using the inverse operation.

22. $^-34 \times {}^+15 = ?$

23. $^-12 \times {}^-23 = ?$

24. $^+532 \div {}^-7 = ?$

25. $^-777 \div {}^-37 = ?$

26. **a.** Suppose the temperature changes by an average of $^-7°$ per hour. Write an equation you can use to determine the temperature change, C, after H hours.

   b. Use your equation to find the temperature change after 3 hours.

   c. How many hours will it take for the temperature to change by $^-42°$?

27. The list below gives average temperatures (in °C) for Fairbanks, Alaska, for each month of the year from January through December. What is the mean of these monthly temperatures?

$^-25, {}^-20, {}^-13, {}^-2, {}^+9, {}^+15, {}^+17, {}^+14, {}^+7, {}^-4, {}^-16, {}^-23$

28. The R-80 Trucking Company carried freight along interstate 80 from New York City to San Francisco. The home base of R-80 Trucking was in Omaha, Nebraska, which is roughly midway between the ends of its line. R-80 truckers averaged about 50 miles per hour on this route, allowing time for rest stops.

R-80 Trucking Company Route Map

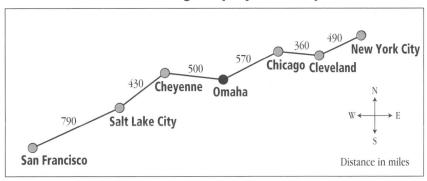

a. Make a number line to represent this truck route. Put Omaha at 0, and use positive numbers for cities east of Omaha and negative numbers for cities west of Omaha.

b. A truck left Omaha, heading east, and traveled for 7 hours. About how far did the truck go? Where on the number line did it stop? Show all your calculations.

c. A truck left Omaha, heading west, and traveled for 4.5 hours. About how far did the truck go? Where on the number line did it stop? Show all your calculations.

d. A truck heading east arrived in Omaha. About where on the number line was the truck 12 hours before it reached Omaha? Show all your calculations.

e. A truck heading west arrived in Omaha. About where on the number line was the truck 11 hours before it reached Omaha? Show all your calculations.

29. The list below shows the yards gained and lost on each play by the Mathville Mudhens in the fourth quarter of their last football game. What was their average gain or loss per play?

$^{-}8, 20, 3, 7, ^{-}15, 4, ^{-}12, 32, 5, 1$

In 30 and 31, write a set of number sentences that shows the related multiplication and division facts for the set of integers. For example, for the integers 27, 9, and 3, the sentences would be

$$9 \times 3 = 27 \qquad 3 = 27 \div 9 \qquad 9 = 27 \div 3$$

30. $7, ^{-}3$, and $^{-}21$

31. $^{-}4, ^{-}5$, and 20

32. Without actually multiplying, how can you decide whether the product of two integers is

   a. positive

   b. negative

   c. 0

33. Without actually dividing, how can you decide whether the quotient of two integers is

   a. positive

   b. negative

   c. 0

Extensions

34. Make a Sum Game with a 6-by-6 grid of sums. Each sum in the grid must be the sum of two integers (addends) listed below the grid.

In 35–38, use the following information: Many towns and small cities have water towers to store water and help maintain water pressure. Water flows into and out of the towers all day long. Generally, flow out of the tower is greatest during the hours when most people are awake and active. The flow into the towers is greatest at night when most people are asleep.

35. If water flows into a tower at the rate of 5000 gallons per hour, how will the supply in the tower change over a 4-hour period? Assume no water flows out of the tower during this time. Show your calculations.

36. If water flows into a tower at the rate of 4000 gallons per hour for a 7-hour period, by how much will the supply at the end of the 7 hours differ from the supply at the beginning of the 7 hours? Assume no water flows out of the tower during this time. Show your calculations.

37. If water flows out of a tower at the rate of 7500 gallons per hour, how will the supply in the tower change over a 3-hour period? Assume no water flows into the tower during this time. Show your calculations.

38. If water flows out of a tower at the rate of 5000 gallons per hour for a 6.5-hour period, by how much will the supply at the end of the 6.5 hours differ from the supply at the beginning of the 6.5-hour period? Assume no water flows into the tower during this time. Show your calculations.

Mathematical Reflections

In this investigation, you explored the multiplication and division of integers. These questions will help you summarize what you have learned:

1 Write a strategy for multiplying two integers. Be sure to consider all possible combinations of positive integers, negative integers, and 0. Verify your strategy by finding the following products.

a. $^-13 \times 7$ **b.** $11 \times ^-20$

c. $^-12 \times 0$ **d.** $^-18 \times ^-22$

2 Write a strategy for dividing two integers. Be sure to consider all possible combinations of positive integers, negative integers, and 0. Verify your strategy by finding the following quotients.

a. $126 \div ^-9$ **b.** $^-36 \div ^-12$

c. $^-2592 \div 32$ **d.** $0 \div 18$

Think about your answers to these questions, discuss your ideas with other students and your teacher, and then write a summary of your findings in your journal.

Coordinate Grids

In previous units, you created and studied coordinate graphs. Coordinate graphs let you look at the relationship between two variables and observe how a change in one variable affects the other variable. All the points on the graphs you have worked with so far have had coordinates greater than or equal to 0. In this investigation, you will see how the coordinate grid can be extended in order to plot points with negative coordinates.

5.1 Extending the Coordinate Grid

The x-axis on a coordinate grid is a horizontal number line, and the y-axis is a vertical number line. On the coordinate grids you have worked with so far, all the values on the x- and y-axes have been greater than or equal to 0.

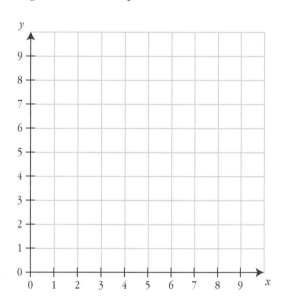

Just as we extended the number line in Investigation 1 to include negative numbers, we can extend the *x*- and *y*-axes of the coordinate grid to include negative numbers.

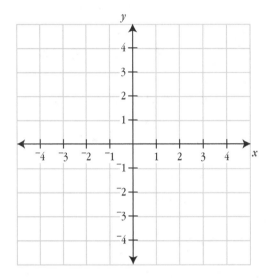

When the axes are extended, they divide the grid into four regions called *quadrants*. We can number these quadrants, starting with the region at the upper right and continuing counterclockwise. The quadrants are usually numbered by using roman numerals as shown below.

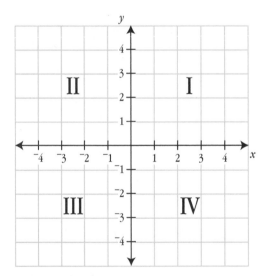

Melina made a coordinate grid and plotted the points (4, 3), (⁻3, 1), (⁻4, ⁻5), and (3, ⁻3). Study her work, and see if you can figure out what she did.

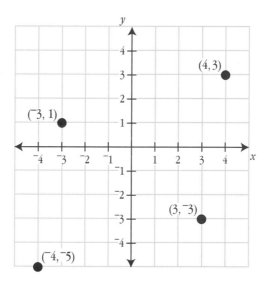

Recall that the two numbers that describe a point are called the *coordinates* of the point. The first number is the *x-coordinate*, and the second number is the *y-coordinate*. For example, the first point Melina plotted has coordinates (4, 3); the *x*-coordinate is 4, and the *y*-coordinate is 3.

Problem 5.1

A. Describe how Melina located each of the four points on the coordinate grid.

B. What polygon could you make by connecting the four points? Justify your answer.

C. On a coordinate grid, plot four points that are the vertices of a square, such that both coordinates of each point are positive integers.

D. On a coordinate grid, plot four points that are the vertices of a square, such that both coordinates of each point are negative integers.

E. On a coordinate grid, plot four points that are the vertices of a square, such that one point has two negative-integer coordinates, one point has two positive-integer coordinates, and each of the other points has one positive-integer coordinate and one negative-integer coordinate.

F. Two vertices of a square are (3, 1) and (⁻1, 1). Find the coordinates for every pair of points that could be the other two vertices.

■ Problem 5.1 Follow-Up

Imagine that you can walk on a coordinate grid. Each integer unit is one step, and you must stay on the grid lines. Suppose you want to walk from point (4, 2) to point (2, 1), taking the least number of steps possible.

You could go 2 steps to the left and then 1 step down.

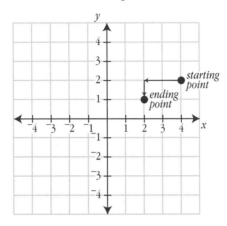

Or you could go 1 step down and then 2 steps to the left.

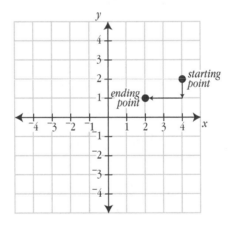

Paths between two points that require the least possible number of steps are called *minimal paths.*

1. For each pairs of points, describe two minimal paths from the first point to the second point.
    a. (⁻4, ⁻2) to (5, 3)   **b.** (⁻4, 3) to (5, 2)   **c.** (2, ⁻4) to (⁻1, ⁻2)

2. **a.** Locate two points on the coordinate grid such that it will take 12 steps to travel from one of the points to the other on a minimal path.
    b. Will everyone name the same two points for part a? Why do you think this is so?

5.2 Breaking Even

Jean is planning to start a bicycle tune-up business. She figures out that her start-up costs will be $800 to buy the tools and parts she needs. She decides to charge $60 for each tune-up. She comes up with the following equation to determine her profit:

$$P = 60t - 800$$

where P is her profit in dollars, and t is the number of tune-ups.

If she does 30 tune-ups ($t = 30$), her profit will be

$$P = (60 \times 30) - 800 = \$1000$$

Jean wants to use her equation to calculate her *break-even point*. That is, she wants to find out the number of tune-ups she will have to do before she begins to make a profit. Then, she wants to figure out how her profit will change with each tune-up after this break-even point.

Problem 5.2

A. Make a table that shows the profit Jean will earn for 0 through 20 tune-ups.

B. Plot the (tune-ups, profit) data from your table on a coordinate grid. Be sure to label the axes. Explain how you chose the scale for each axis.

C. What will Jean's profit be if she does only four tune-ups? How is this shown on the graph?

D. How many tune-ups will Jean have to do before she breaks even? How is this shown on the graph?

E. How does Jean's profit change with each tune-up she does? How is this shown on the graph?

■ **Problem 5.2 Follow-Up**

1. Jean figures out that she could decrease her start-up cost to $600 by buying used tools. She writes a new equation, $P = 60t - 600$, to determine her profit. What is the break-even point for this profit equation?

2. Jean's friend Chuck thinks Jean should advertise her business in the local paper. This would increase her costs, giving her the profit equation $P = 60t - 1200$. What is the break-even point for this profit equation?

5.3 Using a Calculator to Explore Lines

Jean has several profit equations, each based on a different start-up cost. She borrows her brother's graphing calculator so she can explore the graphs of the equations. Since she has never used the calculator before, she decides to start by experimenting with some simple equations.

Problem 5.3

A. 1. Enter the equation $y = 4x$ into your graphing calculator as Y_1, and then press GRAPH to see a graph of the equation. Make a sketch of the graph you see.

2. Predict how the graph of $y = {}^-4x$ will differ from the graph of $y = 4x$. Then, enter the equation $y = {}^-4x$ as Y_2, and press GRAPH to see the graphs of both equations in the same window. Add a sketch of $y = {}^-4x$ to your sketch from part 1.

3. How are the graphs alike? How are they different?

B. 1. Press TABLE to look at the table showing data for both equations ($y = 4x$ and $y = -4x$). You may need to use the ▶ key to see the Y_2 column. Copy part of the table onto your paper.

2. For each value of x in the table, look at the two corresponding values of y (Y_1 and Y_2). How are the two y values for a given x value related? How does this relationship show up in the graph?

C. With your graphing calculator, experiment with each set of equations. Look at the graphs and the tables. Record your observations.

1. $y = 4x + 5$ and $y = {}^-4x + 5$

2. $y = 4x - 5$ and $y = {}^-4x - 5$

■ Problem 5.3 Follow-Up

In 1–3, predict what the graphs of the equations will look like. Then test your predictions by using a graphing calculator.

1. $y = 3x$ and $y = {}^-3x$

2. $y = 3x + 3$ and $y = {}^-3x + 3$

3. $y = 3x - 3$ and $y = {}^-3x - 3$

4. Give three other pairs of equations that will have a relationship similar to the pairs above.

5.4 Exploring Window Settings

Jean's brother tells her that she can change the section of the graph displayed on the calculator by using the ⎡WINDOW⎤ key. Jean decides to experiment with this key, using the equation $y = 3x + 2$.

Below are the window settings Jean used. You will need to refer to these settings as you work on Problem 5.4.

Window settings 1

```
WINDOW
 XMIN=0
 XMAX=10
 XSCL=1
 YMIN=0
 YMAX=10
 YSCL=1
```

Window settings 2

```
WINDOW
 XMIN=⁻10
 XMAX=10
 XSCL=1
 YMIN=⁻10
 YMAX=10
 YSCL=1
```

Problem 5.4

A. On paper, make a table of x and y values for the equation $y = 3x + 2$.

B. On grid paper, sketch a graph of $y = 3x + 2$.

C. Enter the equation $y = 3x + 2$ into your graphing calculator, and press GRAPH . Make a sketch of the graph you see. How does this graph compare with the graph you drew by hand?

D. If you press WINDOW , you will see a screen that allows you to change the section of the graph displayed in the window. Change the settings to those shown in "Window settings 1" on the previous page, and then press GRAPH to see the graph of $y = 3x + 2$ in the new window.

1. Make a sketch of the graph you see.

2. How does this graph compare with the graph you drew by hand in part B?

3. How does this graph compare with the graph you made with your calculator in part C?

4. Explain what you think each entry on the "Window settings 1" screen means.

E. On paper, make a table of x and y values for the equation $y = 2x$.

F. On grid paper, sketch a graph of $y = 2x$.

G. Enter the equation $y = 2x$ into your graphing calculator, and press GRAPH . Make a sketch of the graph you see.

H. Change the window settings to those shown in "Window settings 2" on the previous page, and then press GRAPH to see the graph of $y = 2x$ in the new window.

1. Make a sketch of the graph you see.

2. How does this graph compare with the graph you drew by hand in part F?

3. How does this graph compare with the graph you made with your calculator in part G?

4. Explain what you think each entry on the "Window settings 2" screen means.

Problem 5.4 Follow-Up

1. In part D of Problem 5.4, what happened to the coordinate grid on your calculator when you changed the window settings? Why?

2. Change the window settings so that only quadrant III of the coordinate grid is displayed. Record the window settings you used.

3. Graph $y = 2x$ in this new window. Make a sketch of the graph you see.

4. Except for the point (0,0), which quadrants contain none of the points on the graph of $y = 2x$?

5. Which window settings would you use to display only quadrant II? Quadrant IV?

5.5 Revisiting Jean's Problem

Jean uses her brother's graphing calculator to display the graph of her original profit equation, $P = 60t - 800$. She lets the number of tune-ups, t, be the x variable and the profit, P, be the y variable. She uses the window settings shown below at the left and gets the display shown below at the right.

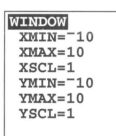
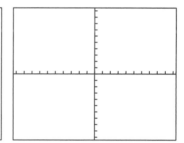

Only the axes appear in the display. There is no sign of the graph anywhere! Jean reasons that the window shown on the screen does not include any of the points on her graph. She needs to change her window settings so that the graph of her equation will show.

Think about this!

What information could Jean use to help her choose an appropriate window setting?

Problem 5.5

In the following questions, use Jean's profit equation $P = 60t - 800$ and your work from Problem 5.2.

A. 1. In the table of data you made in Problem 5.2, what range of values did you use for the number of tune-ups?

2. What range of values did you use for the profit?

B. Enter Jean's profit equation into your calculator. Use the number of tune-ups as the x variable and the profit as the y variable. Use your answers to part A to help you decide how to adjust the window settings so that you will be able to see the graph of the profit equation. Press $\boxed{\text{GRAPH}}$ to display the graph. Make a sketch of the graph you see on the screen.

C. How is the break-even point shown on the graph?

D. Look at the table of data on your calculator. How is the break-even point shown in the table?

■ **Problem 5.5 Follow-Up**

1. Recall that Jean wrote the equation $P = 60t - 600$ to represent the profit she would make if she bought used tools instead of new tools. Find an appropriate window for viewing the graph of this profit equation. Graph the equation on a calculator. Make a sketch of what you see.

2. Jean wrote the equation $P = 60t - 1200$ to represent the profit she would make if she advertised in the local paper. Find an appropriate window for viewing the graph of this profit equation. Graph the equation on a calculator. Make a sketch of what you see.

3. Find the break-even points for the equations in 1 and 2.

As you work on these ACE questions, use your calculator whenever you need it.

Applications

1. a. When the window settings on the left are used, the coordinate axes look like those shown on the right. Copy the axes, and label the tick marks with the appropriate scale values.

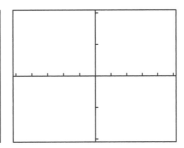

```
WINDOW
 XMIN=⁻10
 XMAX=10
 XSCL=2
 YMIN=⁻10
 YMAX=10
 YSCL=5
```

b. Sketch a graph of the equation $y = {}^-2x$ on the axes.

In 2–5, use the coordinates of the points to figure out what scale interval was used on each axis.

2.

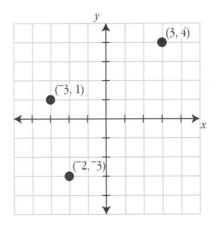

3.

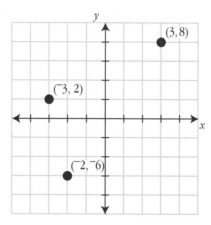

4.

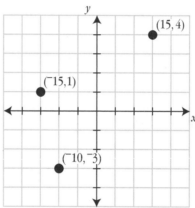

5.

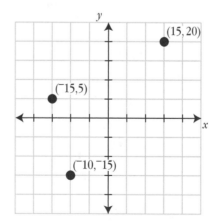

6. The graph at the right shows the relationship between the number of riders on a bike tour and the cost of providing snacks for the riders.

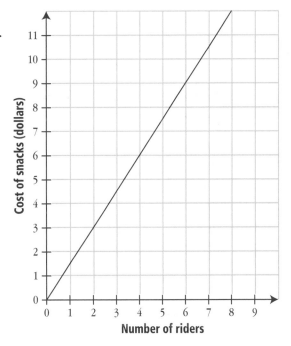

Cost of snacks (dollars)

Number of riders

a. What is the cost of a snack for one rider?

b. What is the total cost of snacks for eight riders?

c. If snacks for all the riders cost $18, how many riders are there?

d. If there were 100 riders, what would be the total cost for the snacks? Explain how you got your answer.

In 7–10, tell which graph on the screen on the left below matches the equation, and explain how you know you are right. The screen on the right shows the settings that were used for the display window.

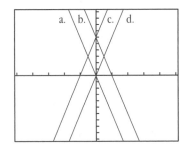

```
WINDOW
  XMIN=⁻5
  XMAX=5
  XSCL=1
  YMIN=⁻10
  YMAX=10
  YSCL=1
```

7. $y = 5x$

8. $y = {}^-5x$

9. $y = 5x + 6$

10. $y = {}^-5x + 6$

Connections

11. Explain why $85 - 73$ is equivalent to $85 + {}^-73$.

12. Three students—Sami, Manoj, and Aimee—started a lawn-mowing business. They made this table and graph to relate their income in dollars (the y values) to the number of weeks worked (the x values). The third screen shows the window settings they used for the graph.

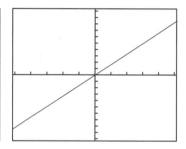

X	Y1
1	80
2	160
3	240
4	320
5	400
6	480

X=1

```
WINDOW
 XMIN=⁻10
 XMAX=10
 XSCL=2
 YMIN=⁻1000
 YMAX=1000
 YSCL=100
```

a. How much income would the students make if they worked 0 weeks? How is this shown on the graph?

b. Locate the point $(^-2, ^-160)$ on the graph. What does this point represent in the context of the situation presented? Is this situation possible? Explain your thinking.

13. The following table gives the temperature (in °C) in Fairbanks, Alaska, for each month over two consecutive years.

Month	Temperature in year 1 (°C)	Temperature in year 2 (°C)
January	−25	−27
February	−20	−23
March	−13	−12
April	−2	−4
May	+9	+10
June	+15	+12
July	+17	+15
August	+14	+16
September	+7	+9
October	−4	0
November	−16	−16
December	−23	−23

a. Find the median and mean temperatures for these two years.

b. Make a coordinate graph that shows how the temperature changed over these two years.

Extensions

14. a. Name five pairs of numbers with a sum of −3.

b. Plot the pairs of numbers from part a, and connect the points.

c. Find the coordinates of a point on the connecting line. (Choose a point that is different from the points you plotted in part b.) What is the sum of these coordinates? Pick another point on the line and find the sum of its coordinates. If you picked a third point on this line, what do you think the sum of its coordinates would be?

d. What would a graph of pairs of numbers whose sum is +8 look like? Justify your answer.

Mathematical Reflections

In this investigation, you extended the coordinate grid to include points with negative coordinates, and you used your graphing calculator to explore graphs of equations. These questions will help you summarize what you have learned:

1 How can you tell which quadrant a point will fall in by looking at its coordinates?

2 You have looked at several problem situations in which you figured out how to make a table of data. You also learned that if you can write an equation to describe how the variables are related, you can use a graphing calculator to graph the equation. How do you figure out what part of the entire graph actually makes sense in the real problem situation? Use an example to help explain.

Think about your answers to these questions, discuss your ideas with other students and your teacher, and then write a summary of your findings in your journal.

Looking Back and Looking Ahead

Unit Reflections

While working on problems in this unit, you investigated properties, operations, and applications of *positive* and *negative* numbers and zero. The numbers {... , −3, −2, −1, 0, 1, 2, 3, ... } are called the *integers*. You learned how to represent integers on a number line and how to add, subtract, multiply, and divide integers. Answering questions about thermometers, distance on a number line, elevations, and scoring games focused your attention on important uses of integers.

Using Your Understanding of Integers — To test your understanding and skill in use of integers, consider the questions that arise in the following games and problem situations.

1 *Kaylee and Cassie designed a board game that involves a number line. In their game, players take turns flipping a penny and moving a marker to the left or the right on a number line like this one.*

These are the rules of the game.

- *At the start of the game each player puts a marker on the point labeled 0.*
- *In round one each player flips a coin and moves 2 spaces to the left if the penny shows a tail (T) or two spaces to the right if the penny shows a head (H).*
- *In round two, each player flips the coin but moves 5 spaces left (T) or right (H).*
- *In round three, each player flips the coin but moves 10 spaces left (T) or right (H).*
- *At the end of three rounds, the player whose marker is on the greater number wins.*

a. Where will Jose's marker end up if he flips HHT on his three turns?

b. Where will Maria's marker end up if she flips THT on her three turns?

c. Consider the possible outcomes of this game and their probabilities.

i. Make a list showing all possible final numbers in the game.

ii. Write number sentences using integer addition to confirm your answers.

iii. Find the probability of ending on each possible final number.

d. Repeat the directions of part c. to show what will happen if the moves in each round are 2, 4, and 6 spaces to the left or right.

2 *Write number sentences involving integer operations that answer the following questions.*

a. In four plays of a football game, one team gained 12 yards, lost 8 yards, lost 3 yards, and gained 7 yards. What was the team's net gain or loss for those four plays?

b. Bill and Susan were comparing the depths of two submarines. One was 890 feet below sea level, and the other was 1425 feet below sea level.

i. Which submarine was at the greater depth?

ii. What change in the first submarine's depth would put it at the same depth as the other submarine?

c. The Blue Devil Booster Club sells snacks at Duke Middle School activities. To get a good price on supplies, the club ordered food worth $125 for each of eight major events and paid in full at the start of the year. After the first four events, the club's total income was $745. How much profit or loss did they have at that time?

d. In Mooseville, the high temperature on one Monday in January was 40°F. It rose 12°F on Tuesday, dropped 10°F on Wednesday, dropped another 6°F on Thursday, and rose 12°F on Friday. What was the high temperature on Friday?

e. Sunday was a cold day in Wolfville. Then the low temperature dropped an average of 8°F per day for the next five days. On Friday, the low temperature was −30°F. What had the low temperature been on Sunday?

3 **a.** Copy and complete the pyramid below so that each number represents the sum of the two numbers directly beneath it.

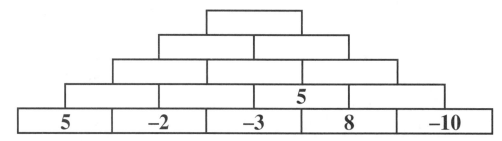

b. Copy and complete the pyramid below so that each number represents the product of the two numbers directly beneath it.

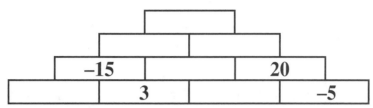

Explaining Your Reasoning—Prior to this unit, you worked only with whole numbers and positive fractions and decimals. Answering the questions in Problems 1–3 required knowledge of integers and operations with integers. You should be able to justify the ways that you used that knowledge in each problem.

1. What operation(s) can you do with the set of integers that you could not do with just the set of whole numbers?

2. Arrange the following numbers from least to greatest and be prepared to justify your answer.

$$-20, \qquad 15, \qquad -55, \qquad 30, \qquad 0$$

3. Use sketches of number line or chip models to demonstrate each of these calculations:

    a. $5 + (-7) = -2$ **b.** $(-2) + (-9) = -11$ **c.** $3 \times (-2) = -6$

    d. $(-3) \times (-2) = 6$

4. If you are given two integers, how do you find the sign of their

    a. sum?

    b. difference?

    c. product?

    d. quotient?

Positive and negative numbers are useful in solving a variety of problems that involve losses and gains. They also provide coordinates for points on an extended number line and coordinate plane. These ideas will be useful when you study graphs of functions in future *Connected Mathematics* units like *Moving Straight Ahead*, *Thinking with Mathematical Models*, and *Growing, Growing, Growing*. You will also use negative and positive numbers when you solve equations in these units and in the algebraic reasoning of *Say It with Symbols*.

absolute value The absolute value of a number is its distance from 0 on a number line. It can be thought of as the value of a number when its sign is ignored. For example, ⁻3 and 3 both have an absolute value of 3.

integers The whole numbers and their opposites. 0 is an integer, but it is neither positive nor negative. The integers from ⁻4 to 4 are shown on the number line below.

inverse operations Operations that "undo" each other. Addition and subtraction are inverse operations. For example, the subtraction equation $7 - 4 = 3$ is undone by the addition equation $3 + 4 = 7$. Multiplication and division are inverse operations. For example, for multiplication equation $2 \times 6 = 12$ is undone by the division equations $12 \div 2 = 6$ and $12 \div 6 = 2$.

negative number A number less than 0. On a number line, negative numbers are located to the left of 0 (on a vertical number line, negative numbers are located below 0).

number sentence A mathematical statement that gives the relationship between two expressions, which are composed of numbers and operation signs. For example, $3 + 2 = 5$ and $6 \times 2 > 10$ are number sentences; $3 + 2$, 5, 6×2, and 10 are expressions.

opposites Two numbers whose sum is 0. For example, ⁻3 and 3 are opposites. On a number line, opposites are the same distance from 0 but in different directions from 0. The number 0 is its own opposite.

positive number A number greater than 0. (The number 0 is neither positive nor negative.) On a number line, positive numbers are located to the right of 0 (on a vertical number line, positive numbers are located above 0).

quadrants The four sections into which the coordinate plane is divided by the *x*- and *y*-axes. The quadrants are labeled as follows:

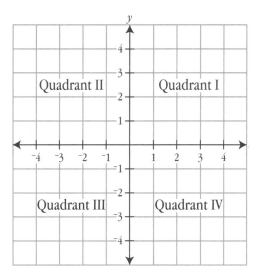

Glosario

cuadrantes Las cuatro secciones en las que un plano de coordenadas queda dividido por los ejes *x* e *y*. Los cuadrantes se identifican de la siguiente manera:

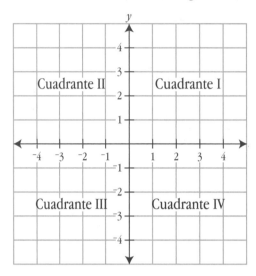

enteros Números enteros positivos y sus opuestos. 0 es un entero, pero no es ni positivo ni negativo. En la siguiente recta numérica figuran los enteros comprendidos entre ⁻4 y 4.

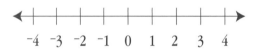

número negativo Un número menor que 0. En una recta numérica, los números negativos están ubicados a la izquierda de 0 (en una recta numérica vertical, los números negativos están ubicados debajo de 0).

número positivo Un número mayor que 0. (El número 0 no es ni positivo ni negativo.) En una recta numérica los números positivos se ubican a la derecha de 0 (en una recta numérica vertical, los números positivos están por encima de 0).

operaciones inversas Operaciones que se "anulan" mutuamente. Por ejemplo, la ecuación de resta $7 - 4 = 3$ queda anulada por la ecuación de suma $3 + 4 = 7$. La multiplicación y la división son operaciones inversas. Por ejemplo, la ecuación de multiplicación $2 \times 6 = 12$ queda anulada por las ecuaciones de división $12 \div 2 = 6$ y $12 \div 6 = 2$.

opuestos Dos números cuya suma da 0. Por ejemplo, $^-3$ y 3 son opuestos. En una recta numérica, los opuestos se encuentran a la misma distancia de 0 pero en distintos sentidos. El número 0 es su propio opuesto.

oración numérica Un enunciado matemático que describe la relación entre dos expresiones compuestas por números y signos de operaciones. Por ejemplo, $3 + 2 = 5$ y $6 \times 2 > 10$ son oraciones numéricas. $3 + 2$, 5, 6×2 y 10 son expresiones.

valor absoluto El valor absoluto de un número es su distancia de 0 sobre una recta numérica. Se puede interpretar como el valor de un número cuando no importa su signo. Por ejemplo, tanto $^-3$ como 3 tienen un valor absoluto de 3.

Index